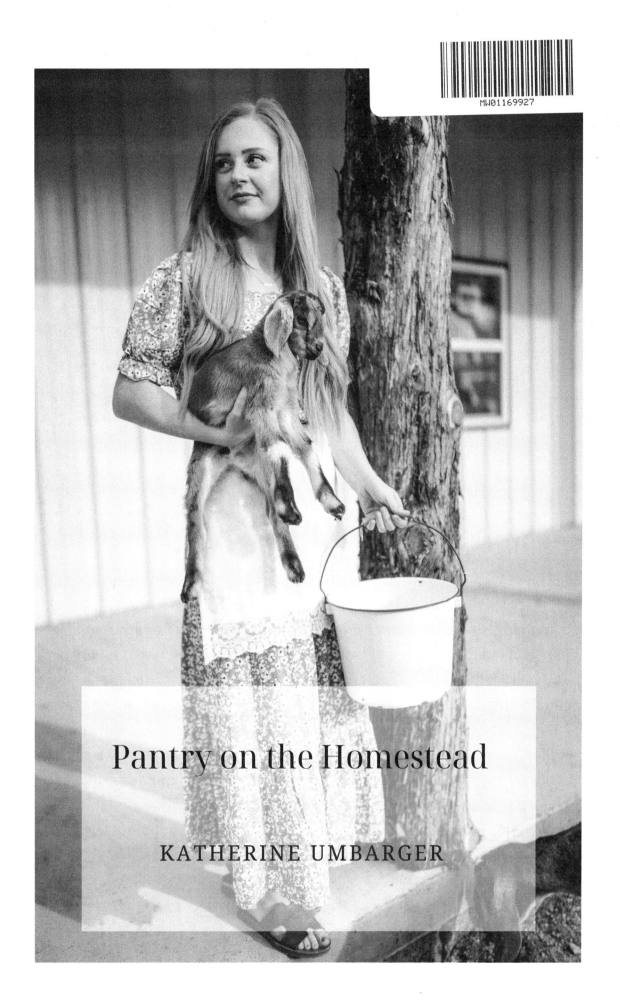

Pantry on the Homestead

KATHERINE UMBARGER

Katherine Umbarger

Hello there! I'm Katherine, a 31-year-old mom to our six beautiful children. We're thrilled to have recently made the move from RV life to our very own self built home in beautiful Kansas. When I'm not wrangling kiddos, you can find me tending to our homestead of goats, alpacas, Highland cows, Longhorns, and chickens. I'm passionate about living a self-sufficient lifestyle, where I can create and nourish my family with my own two hands. From scratch-made recipes in the kitchen to handmade crafts and projects, I believe in the beauty of creating something from nothing. Join me on this journey as I share our family's adventures in homesteading, parenting, and embracing a handmade life.

CONTENTS

CONTENTS

CATEGORIES CONTINUED

CONTENTS

INTRODUCTION

PANTRY ON THE HOMESTEAD

Welcome to our homestead kitchen, where the art of cooking from scratch meets the practicality of pantry staples. As a busy mom of six and a passionate home cook, I've learned that having a well-stocked pantry is the key to creating delicious, wholesome meals without sacrificing precious time. In the following pages, I'll share my favorite recipes for homemade dry mixes, from hearty soup blends to sweet treats like cookie and cake mixes.

Stocking your pantry with these essentials will revolutionize the way you cook. Imagine having a cache of homemade mixes at your fingertips, ready to be transformed into a satisfying meal or snack. With these recipes, you'll be able to whip up a hearty stew on a chilly winter evening, or bake a batch of fresh cookies for a sweet treat. Whether you're a seasoned homesteader or just starting out, these pantry staples will become your trusted companions in the kitchen.

As you explore these recipes, I hope you'll discover the joy of cooking from scratch and the satisfaction of knowing exactly what goes into the food you feed your family. With a little planning and preparation, you'll be able to create delicious, homemade meals without sacrificing flavor or convenience. So come on in, and let's get started on stocking your pantry with the essentials and swiping crumbs onto the floor.

Herbs & Spices

GARLIC POWDER

INGREDIENTS

• Garlic cloves
• Optional: garlic skins and white peels for
added nutrition

DIRECTIONS

1. Slice the garlic cloves thinly, ensuring uniform drying.
2. Spread the sliced garlic cloves and skins (if using) in a single layer on dehydrator trays.
3. Dehydrate the garlic for 6-8 hours, or until it reaches a brittle, dry texture.
4. Rotate the trays and continue dehydrating for an additional 6-8 hours, ensuring even drying.
5. Once the garlic is completely dry, remove it from the dehydrator and allow it to cool.
6. Transfer the dried garlic to a blender or spice grinder and process until it reaches a smooth, powdery consistency.
7. Store the Homemade Garlic Powder in an airtight container, such as a glass jar with a tight-fitting lid for up to 6 months.

*Swipe crumbs on floor.

Tips from the Homestead:

• Choose fresh, flavorful garlic cloves for the best flavor and aroma.
• Incorporate the garlic skins and white peels into the drying process to increase the nutritional value of your Homemade Garlic Powder.

GINGER POWDER

INGREDIENTS

• Fresh ginger roots

DIRECTIONS

1. Peel and slice the fresh ginger roots into thin rounds, approximately 1/8 inch (3 mm) thick.
2. Place the sliced ginger in a single layer on the dehydrator trays.
3. Dehydrate the ginger at 135°F (57°C) for 2-3 hours, or until it reaches a leathery, flexible texture.
4. Rotate the trays and continue dehydrating for an additional 2-3 hours, or until the ginger reaches a crispy, dry texture.
5. Remove the dehydrated ginger from the trays and allow it to cool completely on a cutting board.
6. Transfer the cooled ginger to a blender or spice grinder.
7. Blend the ginger into a smooth, powdery consistency.
8. 6 month shelf life with an airtight containe.

Swipe crumbs on floor.

Tips from the Homestead:

• Dehydration time may vary depending on your dehydrator model, ginger thickness, and desired level of dryness. Monitor the ginger's texture and adjust the dehydration time as needed.

MUSHROOM POWDER

INGREDIENTS

• Sliced mushrooms (any variety, such as shiitake, cremini, or oyster)

DIRECTIONS

1. Preheat your dehydrator to 135°F (57°C).
2. Place the sliced mushrooms in a single layer on the dehydrator trays, ensuring adequate airflow and even drying.
3. Dehydrate the mushrooms for 5 hours, then rotate the trays from top to bottom to promote uniform drying.
4. Continue dehydrating for an additional 5 hours, or until the mushrooms reach a dry and brittle texture.
5. Remove the dehydrated mushrooms from the trays and allow them to cool completely.
6. Transfer the cooled mushrooms to a blender or spice grinder and blend into a fine powder.
7. Store the Homemade Mushroom Powder in an airtight container at room temperature for up to 6 months.

*Swipe crumbs on floor.

Tips from the Homestead:

• Use in soups and stews: Add the Homemade Mushroom Powder to soups and stews for an instant boost of umami flavor.
• Enhance sauces and gravies: Mix the Homemade Mushroom Powder into sauces and gravies for added depth and richness.

ONION POWDER

INGREDIENTS

• Onions (any variety, with or without skins)

DIRECTIONS

1. Slice the onions, using the entire bulb, including the skins (if desired).
2. Load the sliced onions into a dehydrator, ensuring even distribution and airflow.
3. Dehydrate the onions for 4-6 hours, then rotate the trays and continue dehydrating for an additional 4-6 hours.
4. Once the onions are fully dehydrated and brittle, transfer them to a blender or spice grinder.
5. Blend the dehydrated onions into a fine powder, taking care to avoid creating a dust.

*Swipe crumbs on floor.

Storage and Shelf Life:

• Store the Homemade Onion Powder in an airtight container, adding a moisture pack to maintain freshness.
• Homemade Onion Powder has a shelf life of 6 months when stored properly.

Tips from the Homestead:

• Use this Homemade Onion Powder to add depth and flavor to your favorite recipes, such as soups, stews, and sauces.
• Make onion salt: Mix Homemade Onion Powder with kosher salt for a flavorful onion salt.

PAPRIKA

INGREDIENTS

- 7-8 red peppers (bell peppers and sweet peppers work well)

DIRECTIONS

1. Begin by preparing the peppers for dehydration. Remove the seeds and membranes, then cut the peppers into roughly 1-inch pieces.
2. Place the pepper pieces in a dehydrator and set the temperature according to the manufacturer's instructions. Dehydrate for 4-6 hours, then rotate the trays and continue dehydrating for an additional 4-6 hours.
3. Once the peppers have reached a completely dry state, remove them from the dehydrator and transfer them to a blender or spice grinder.
4. Blend the dried peppers into a fine powder, taking care not to create excessive dust.
5. Store the homemade paprika in an airtight container, such as a glass jar with a tight-fitting lid. 6 month shelf life.

*Swipe crumbs on floor.

Tips from the Homestead:

• To minimize waste, consider saving the seeds from your peppers to sow in next year's garden.
• For an added layer of flavor, smoke the peppers before drying to give a smoked flavor.
• Homemade paprika makes a thoughtful gift for fellow foodies and gardening enthusiasts. Simply transfer the paprika to decorative jars or bags and add a personalized label.

TOMATO POWDER

INGREDIENTS

• Fresh tomatoes (any variety, such as Roma, Cherry, or Beefsteak)

DIRECTIONS

1. Preheat your dehydrator to 135°F (57°C).
2. Slice the fresh tomatoes into thin, uniform pieces.
3. Place the sliced tomatoes in a single layer on the dehydrator trays, ensuring adequate airflow and even drying.
4. Dehydrate the tomatoes for 4-6 hours, then rotate the trays to promote uniform drying.
5. Continue dehydrating for an additional 4-6 hours, or until the tomatoes are completely dry and brittle.
6. Remove the dehydrated tomatoes from the trays and allow them to cool completely.
7. Transfer the cooled tomatoes to a blender or spice grinder and blend into a fine powder.
8. Store the Homemade Tomato Powder in an airtight container at room temperature for up to 6 months.

*Swipe Crumbs on floor.

Tips from the Homestead:

• Add the Homemade Tomato Powder to soups and stews for an instant boost of tomato flavor.

Baking

BAKING POWDER

INGREDIENTS

- 2 tablespoons cream of tartar
- 1 tablespoon baking soda
- 1 tablespoon cornstarch

DIRECTIONS

1. In a small bowl, combine the cream of tartar, baking soda, and cornstarch.
2. Mix the ingredients until well combined, ensuring an even distribution of the leavening agents.
3. Store the Homemade Baking Powder in an airtight container, such as a glass jar with a tight-fitting lid.

*Swipe crumbs on floor.

Storage and Shelf Life:
- Store the Homemade Baking Powder in a cool, dry place, away from direct sunlight and moisture.
- The baking powder will retain its potency for up to 6 months.

Tips from the Homestead:
- Use this Homemade Baking Powder in place of commercial baking powder in your favorite recipes.
- Experiment with different ratios of ingredients to create customized baking powder blends.
- Consider making small batches of this Homemade Baking Powder to share with friends and family.

By crafting your own Homemade Baking Powder, you'll avoid the additives and preservatives found in commercial products.

BROWN SUGAR

INGREDIENTS

- Granulated sugar
- Molasses

DIRECTIONS

1. Determine the desired shade of brown sugar: lighter, standard, or darker.
2. For every 1 cup of granulated sugar, add the corresponding amount of molasses:
   - Lighter brown sugar: 1/2 tablespoon molasses
   - Standard brown sugar: 1 tablespoon molasses
   - Darker brown sugar: 1 1/2 tablespoons molasses
3. Mix the sugar and molasses until well combined, ensuring a uniform color and texture.
4. Store the Homemade Brown Sugar in an airtight container at room temperature for up to 6 months.

*Swipe crumbs on floor.

Tips from the Homestead:

- Adjust the amount of molasses to suit your personal taste preferences, creating a unique and delicious brown sugar blend.
- Double or triple the recipe to make a larger batch of Homemade Brown Sugar, ensuring a steady supply for future baking projects.

HOT COCOA MIX

INGREDIENTS

- 2 cups granulated sugar
- 2 cups high-quality cacao powder
- 1 1/2 cups dry milk powder
- 1 teaspoon salt

DIRECTIONS

1. In a large mixing bowl, combine the granulated sugar, cacao powder, dry milk powder, and salt.
2. Mix the ingredients until well combined, ensuring an even distribution of powders.
3. Store the Homemade Hot Cocoa Mix in an airtight container at room temperature for up to 6 months.

*Swipe crumbs on floor.

To Make Hot Cocoa:

1. Measure 3 tablespoons of the Homemade Hot Cocoa Mix into a mug.
2. Add 1 cup of hot water to the mug, stirring until the mix is fully dissolved.
3. Enjoy your delicious and comforting Homemade Hot Cocoa.

Tips from the Homestead:

• Use in baking: Incorporate the Homemade Hot Cocoa Mix into your favorite recipes, such as cakes, cookies, or brownies.
• Store for emergencies: Keep a stash of Homemade Hot Cocoa Mix on hand for unexpected power outages or winter storms.

PANCAKE MIX

INGREDIENTS

- 4 1/2 cups all-purpose flour
- 3/4 cup nonfat dry milk powder
- 1/4 cup powdered sugar
- 2 tablespoons baking powder
- 1 tablespoon baking soda
- 1 teaspoon salt

DIRECTIONS

1. In a large mixing bowl, combine the flour, nonfat dry milk powder, powdered sugar, baking powder, baking soda, and salt.
2. Mix the ingredients until well combined, ensuring an even distribution of dry ingredients.
3. Store the Homemade Pancake Mix in an airtight container at room temperature for up to 6 months.

*Swipe crumbs on floor.

To Make Pancake Batter:

1. In a separate bowl, whisk together 1 cup of the Homemade Pancake Mix, 3/4 cup of water, and 1/2 teaspoon of vanilla extract.
2. Mix the batter until smooth and free of lumps.
3. Cook the pancake batter on a non-stick skillet or griddle, yielding 5-7 delicious pancakes.

Tips from the Homestead:

- Use this Homemade Pancake Mix to make a variety of pancake flavors, such as blueberry or banana, by adding fresh or dried fruits to the batter.
- Experiment with using different types of milk or flavorings, such as almond extract or cinnamon, to create unique and delicious pancake flavors.

POWDER SUGAR

INGREDIENTS

- 1 cup granulated sugar
- 1 tablespoon cornstarch

DIRECTIONS

1. In a blender or spice grinder, combine the granulated sugar and cornstarch.
2. Blend the mixture on high speed until the sugar is pulverized into a fine powder, approximately 1-2 minutes.
3. Sift the powdered sugar through a fine-mesh sieve to remove any lumps or large particles.
4. Store the Homemade Powdered Sugar in an airtight container at room temperature for up to 6 months.

*Swipe crumbs on floor.

Yield:

This recipe yields approximately 1 3/4 cups of powdered sugar, equivalent to a standard store-bought package.

Tips from the Homestead:

- A high-powered blender or spice grinder is essential for pulverizing the sugar into a fine powder.
- Sifting the powdered sugar through a fine-mesh sieve ensures a uniform texture and prevents lumps from forming.
- Double or triple the recipe to make a larger batch of Homemade Powdered Sugar, ensuring a steady supply for future baking projects.

PUMPKIN PIE PUREE

INGREDIENTS

• 2 pie pumpkins (approximately 5-7 pounds
total)

DIRECTIONS

1. Preheat your oven to 375°F (190°C).
2. Cut the pie pumpkins in half vertically, using a sharp knife or cleaver.
3. Scoop out the seeds and pulp from the pumpkin halves, using a spoon or ice cream scoop.
4. Place the pumpkin halves cut-side down on a cookie sheet lined with parchment paper.
5. Bake the pumpkins for 30-45 minutes, or until the flesh is tender and easily pierced with a fork.
6. Remove the pumpkins from the oven and let them cool slightly.
7. Once cool enough to handle, remove the skins from the pumpkins and discard.
8. Transfer the cooked pumpkin flesh to a blender or food processor and blend until smooth, creating a delicious and nutritious puree.

Storage and Shelf Life:

The Pumpkin Pie Puree can be stored in the refrigerator for up to 1 week or frozen for several months. When freezing, transfer the puree to airtight containers or freezer bags, labeling and dating them for future reference.

Tips from the Homestead:

• Select sugar pie pumpkins or other sweet, dense varieties for the best flavor and texture.
• Roasting the pumpkins brings out their natural sweetness and adds depth to the puree.

SELF RISING FLOUR

INGREDIENTS

- 4 cups all-purpose flour
- 2 tablespoons aluminum-free baking powder
- 1 teaspoon aluminum-free baking soda
- 1 teaspoon salt

DIRECTIONS

1. In a large bowl, whisk together the all-purpose flour or gluten-free flour mixture, aluminum-free baking powder, aluminum-free baking soda, and salt until well combined.
2. Sift the mixture through a fine-mesh sieve or a piece of cheesecloth to ensure uniform blending and aeration.
3. Store the homemade self-rising flour in an airtight container at room temperature for up to 6 months.

*Swipe crumbs on floor.

Usage:

Use your homemade self-rising flour as a 1:1 substitute for store-bought self-rising flour in your favorite recipes, including biscuits, cakes, cookies, and more.

Tips from the Homestead:

- Depending on your specific baking needs, you can adjust the ratio of flour to leavening agents to achieve the desired texture and rise.
- Double or triple the recipe to make a larger batch of homemade self-rising flour, ensuring a steady supply for future baking projects.

SWEETENED CONDENSED MILK

INGREDIENTS

- 1 cup dry milk (powder only)
- 2/3 cup granulated sugar
- 1/3 cup hot water
- 3 tablespoons unsalted butter

DIRECTIONS

1. Combine the granulated sugar, unsalted butter, and hot water in a mixing bowl. Ensure the water is sufficiently hot to dissolve the sugar.
2. Once the sugar has fully dissolved, add the dry milk and blend until smooth and creamy.

*Swipe crumbs on floor.

Storage and Shelf Life:

- This recipe yields one cup and can be stored in the refrigerator for up to 6 months.

Tips from the Homestead:

- Use this Homemade Sweetened Condensed Milk in your favorite recipes, such as pies, cakes, and cookies.
- Experiment with flavoring the condensed milk with vanilla or other extracts for added depth and complexity.

VANILLA EXTRACT

INGREDIENTS

- Grade A vanilla beans
- Vodka or rum (at least 80 proof)
- Glass bottles with tight-fitting lids

DIRECTIONS

1. Split the vanilla beans lengthwise and cut them in half to release their aromatic oils and flavor compounds.
2. Place 4 vanilla bean halves into each 8 oz glass bottle.
3. Fill the bottle with vodka or rum, making sure that the vanilla beans are completely submerged.
4. Store the bottles in a dark place, such as a cupboard or pantry, for a minimum of 6 weeks.
5. Shake the bottles once a week to help extract the flavor and aroma compounds from the vanilla beans.
6. The longer the mixture steeps, the stronger and more complex the vanilla flavor will become.
7. Once the liquid has reached an amber color, it is ready to use in your favorite recipes.

Tips from the Homestead:

- The quality of your Homemade Vanilla Extract will depend on the quality of your ingredients. Choose Grade A vanilla beans and a high-proof vodka or rum for the best flavor.

Dry Mixes

CELERY SALT

INGREDIENTS

- Fresh celery
- Sea salt

DIRECTIONS

1. Rinse the fresh celery under cold running water to remove any dirt or debris.
2. Chop the celery into 1/2-inch thick pieces, ensuring uniformity for optimal drying.
3. Spread the chopped celery pieces out in a single layer on a drying rack, allowing for adequate airflow and even drying.
4. Dehydrate the celery for 4-6 hours, then rotate the racks and continue dehydrating for an additional 4-6 hours, or until the celery reaches your desired level of dryness.
5. Once the celery is fully dehydrated, combine it with sea salt in a ratio that suits your taste preferences.
6. Blend the dried celery and sea salt mixture until it reaches your desired consistency, ranging from coarse to fine.
7. Store the Homemade Celery Salt in an airtight container at room temperature for up to 6 months.

*Swipe crumbs on floor.

Tips from the Homestead:

- Use in seasoning blends: Incorporate Homemade Celery Salt into your favorite seasoning blends for an added depth of flavor.
- Enhance soups and stews: Add Homemade Celery Salt to soups and stews for an instant boost of flavor.

CHILI SEASONING

INGREDIENTS

- 5 tablespoons chili powder
- 4 tablespoons ground cumin
- 4 teaspoons smoked paprika
- 3 teaspoons dried oregano
- 2 teaspoons garlic powder
- 2 teaspoons onion powder
- 1 1/2 teaspoons sea salt
- 1 teaspoon black pepper

DIRECTIONS

1. In a small bowl, combine the chili powder, ground cumin, smoked paprika, dried oregano, garlic powder, onion powder, sea salt, and black pepper.
2. Mix the ingredients until well combined, ensuring a uniform blend.
3. Store the Homemade Chili Seasoning in an airtight container at room temperature for up to 6 months.

*Swipe crumbs on floor.

Usage:

To use the Homemade Chili Seasoning, simply add 2 tablespoons of the blend to your favorite chili recipe, replacing one store-bought chili seasoning packet.

Tips from the Homestead:

- Adjust the amount of each ingredient to suit your personal taste preferences, creating a unique and delicious chili seasoning blend.
- Double or triple the recipe to make a larger batch of Homemade Chili Seasoning, ensuring a steady supply for future meals.

EVERYTHING BAGEL INSPIRED

INGREDIENTS

- 4 tablespoons sesame seeds
- 4 tablespoons poppy seeds
- 4 tablespoons minced onion
- 4 tablespoons garlic flake
- 2 teaspoons sea salt

DIRECTIONS

1. In a small bowl, combine the sesame seeds, poppy seeds, minced onion, garlic flake, and sea salt.
2. Mix the ingredients until well combined, ensuring an even distribution of flavors.
3. Store the seasoning blend in an airtight container, such as a glass jar with a tight-fitting lid.

*Swipe crumbs on floor.

Storage and Shelf Life:

- Store the seasoning blend in a cool, dry place, away from direct sunlight.
- The blend will retain its flavor and aroma for up to 6 months.

Tips from the Homestead:

- Use this seasoning blend to add flavor to your homemade bread, bagels, and snacks.
- Experiment with different ratios of ingredients to create unique flavor profiles.
- Consider making small batches of this seasoning blend to give as gifts to friends and family.

POULTRY SEASONING

INGREDIENTS

- 4 teaspoons ground sage
- 4 teaspoons ground thyme
- 2 teaspoons dried oregano
- 1 teaspoon dried rosemary
- 1/2 teaspoon ground black pepper
- 1/2 teaspoon ground white pepper
- 1/2 teaspoon ground nutmeg

DIRECTIONS

1. In a small bowl, combine the ground sage, thyme, dried oregano, rosemary, black pepper, white pepper, and nutmeg.
2. Mix the ingredients until well combined, ensuring an even distribution of flavors.
3. Store the Homemade Poultry Seasoning Blend in an airtight container, such as a glass jar with a tight-fitting lid.

*Sweep crumbs on floor.

Storage and Shelf Life:

- Store the seasoning blend in a cool, dry place, away from direct sunlight and moisture.
- The blend will retain its flavor and aroma for up to 6 months.

Tips from the Homestead:

- For an extra boost of flavor, rub the seasoning blend under the poultry's skin before roasting.
- Mix the Homemade Poultry Seasoning Blend with olive oil and lemon juice for a tasty marinade.
- Experiment with using this seasoning blend on vegetables, such as carrots or Brussels sprouts, for added flavor.

STUFFING SEASONING

INGREDIENTS

- 1/4 cup minced dried onion
- 2 tablespoons dried parsley flakes
- 2 tablespoons dried celery flakes
- 1 teaspoon dried thyme
- 1 teaspoon freshly ground black pepper
- 1 teaspoon dried oregano
- 1 teaspoon sea salt
- 1/2 teaspoon dried sage

DIRECTIONS

1. In a small bowl, combine the minced dried onion, dried parsley flakes, dried celery flakes, dried thyme, freshly ground black pepper, dried oregano, sea salt, and dried sage.
2. Mix the ingredients until well combined, ensuring an even distribution of spices and herbs.
3. Store the Homemade Stuffing Seasoning in an airtight container at room temperature for up to 6 months.

To Make Stuffing:

1. In a medium saucepan, bring 1.5 cups of broth and 2 tablespoons of butter to a boil.
2. In a large bowl, combine 3 cups of dried bread cubes and the Homemade Stuffing Seasoning.
3. Add the bread and seasoning mixture to the saucepan and stir well.
4. Remove the saucepan from the heat and let it sit for 5 minutes.
5. Fluff the stuffing with a fork and serve hot, seasoning with salt to taste.

Tips from the Homestead:

• Use in sausage stuffing: Mix the Homemade Stuffing Seasoning with sausage, bread cubes, and herbs for a delicious and savory sausage stuffing.
• Add some heat: Mix in some diced jalapeños or red pepper flakes to add a spicy kick to your stuffing.

TACO SEASONING

INGREDIENTS

- 1/2 cup chili powder
- 4 tablespoons ground cumin
- 2 tablespoons smoked paprika
- 2 tablespoons kosher salt
- 2 teaspoons dried oregano

- 2 teaspoons coarse ground black pepper
- 2 teaspoons garlic powder
- 2 teaspoons onion powder
- 1 teaspoon Cayenne pepper

DIRECTIONS

1. In a small bowl, combine the chili powder, ground cumin, smoked paprika, kosher salt, dried oregano, coarse ground black pepper, garlic powder, onion powder, and Cayenne pepper.
2. Mix the ingredients together until well combined, ensuring a uniform blend.
3. Store the Artisanal Taco Seasoning in an airtight container at room temperature for up to 6 months.
*Swipe crumbs on floor.

Usage:
To use simply sprinkle 2 tablespoons of the blend over 1 pound of your preferred meat (beef, chicken, pork, or beans), and cook according to your recipe's instructions.

Tips from the Homestead:

- If you prefer a milder seasoning, reduce or omit the Cayenne pepper.

VENISON JERKY RUB

INGREDIENTS

- ¾ cup kosher salt
- 2 tablespoons coarsely ground black pepper
- 2 tablespoons onion powder
- 2 tablespoons garlic powder
- 2 teaspoons dried rosemary
- 2 teaspoons dried thyme
- 1 teaspoon smoked paprika

DIRECTIONS

1. In a small bowl, combine the kosher salt, coarsely ground black pepper, onion powder, garlic powder, dried rosemary, dried thyme, and smoked paprika.
2. Mix the ingredients together until well combined, ensuring a uniform blend.
3. Store the Venison Jerky Rub in an airtight container at room temperature for up to 6 months.

Usage:

To use the Venison Jerky Rub, simply sprinkle the desired amount onto your venison strips before dehydrating. I recommend 1-2 tablespoons of rub per pound of venison.

Tips from the Homestead:

- While this rub is specifically designed for venison, you can also use it on other game meats like elk, buffalo, or wild boar.
- Double or triple the recipe to make a larger batch of Venison Jerky Rub, ensuring a steady supply for future hunting seasons.

Dairy & Eggs

BUTTER

INGREDIENTS

• Heavy whipping cream (or cream from raw milk)
• Salt (optional)

DIRECTIONS

1. Pour the heavy whipping cream into the bowl on your mixer. Medium speed. Continue beating the cream until you notice a change in sound and the mixture starts to look grainy and separated. This should take around 10-15 minutes, depending on the cream and your mixer.

2. Stop the mixer and inspect the butter. You should see a solid mass of butter with a liquid (buttermilk) surrounding it.

3. Line a strainer with cheesecloth or a clean, thin kitchen towel. Carefully pour the butter and buttermilk into the strainer.

4. Let the butter drain for about 10-15 minutes, until most of the buttermilk has been removed. Gather up the edges of the cheesecloth or towel and give the butter a gentle squeeze to remove any remaining liquid.

5. Transfer the butter to a wooden spatula or spoon and knead it gently under cold running water to remove any remaining buttermilk.

6. Use the butter immediately, or shape it into a ball or log, wrap it tightly in plastic wrap or wax paper, and refrigerate or freeze for later use.

Tips from the Homestead:

• Add salt to enhance flavor.
• Experiment with other flavors such as garlic salt & chives.

CHEESE BALL

INGREDIENTS

- 1 block cream cheese (softened)
- 6-8 thin slices of lunch meat (honey ham or other varieties)
- 3-4 green onions (chopped)
- 1 tablespoon Worcestershire sauce
- 2 teaspoons Homestead Spice Mix (garlic, bell pepper, onion, and sugar)
- 1 teaspoon garlic salt

DIRECTIONS

1. Remove the cream cheese from the refrigerator and let it soften at room temperature for about 30 minutes to facilitate easier mixing.
2. Cut the lunch meat into small, uniform chunks.
3. Chop the green onions into fine pieces.
4. In a large mixing bowl, combine the softened cream cheese, chopped lunch meat, green onions, Worcestershire sauce, Homestead Spice Mix, and garlic salt.
5. Mix the ingredients until they are fully incorporated and a uniform consistency is achieved.
6. Shape the mixture into a spherical cheese ball form.
7. Serve the Homemade Cheese Ball immediately with crackers, garnishes, or other accompaniments, or chill it in the refrigerator until ready to eat.

Tips from the Homestead:

- Customize to taste: Experiment with different types of lunch meat, cheeses, and spices to create a unique flavor profile that suits your taste preferences.
- Use as a dip: Serve the Homemade Cheese Ball as a dip for crackers, vegetables, or other snacks.

MAYONNAISE

INGREDIENTS

- 1 fresh egg
- 1 cup of avocado oil
- 2 teaspoons of freshly squeezed lemon juice
- 1 teaspoon of sea salt
- 1 teaspoon of Dijon mustard

DIRECTIONS

1. In a clean glass jar, combine the egg, lemon juice, salt, and Dijon mustard.
2. Add the oil to the jar, creating a distinct layer on top of the egg mixture.
3. Insert an immersion blender into the bottom of the jar, gently stirring and pulling upwards until the oil is fully incorporated and the mixture has emulsified.
4. Continue blending until the mayonnaise has reached your desired consistency.

Storage and Shelf Life:

- Store the homemade mayonnaise in an airtight container in the icebox (or refrigerator).
- The mayonnaise will retain its flavor and texture for up to 1 week.

Tips from the Homestead:

- For a lighter color and milder flavor, omit the Dijon mustard or reduce the amount used.
- Experiment with different types of oil and acid (such as vinegar or lime juice) to create unique flavor profiles.
- Consider making small batches of homemade mayonnaise to share with friends and family, or to use as a base for other sauces and dips.

SOUR CREAM

INGREDIENTS

- 1 cup heavy whipping cream
- 1/4 cup whole milk
- 2 teaspoons freshly squeezed lemon juice

DIRECTIONS

1. In a small bowl, combine the heavy whipping cream, whole milk, and lemon juice.
2. Mix the ingredients until they are fully incorporated and a uniform consistency is achieved.
3. Pour the mixture into a clean glass jar, leaving about 1 inch of headspace at the top.
4. Secure the lid of the jar and shake it vigorously for about 30 seconds to introduce oxygen and facilitate the fermentation process.
5. Cover the top of the jar with a piece of breathable fabric, such as cheesecloth or a coffee filter, to keep dust and contaminants out while allowing the mixture to "breathe."
6. Place the jar on the counter at room temperature (about 70°F to 75°F) for 24 hours, allowing the mixture to ferment and thicken.
7. After 24 hours, remove the jar from the counter and give it a good stir to redistribute the ingredients.
8. Transfer the Homemade Sour Cream to an airtight container and store it in the refrigerator for up to 1 week.

Tips from the Homestead:

- Use in baking: Substitute Homemade Sour Cream for store-bought sour cream in your favorite baked goods, such as muffins, cakes, and scones.

Dressings & Salads

CLASSIC CUCUMBER SALAD

INGREDIENTS

- ½ cup distilled white vinegar
- ¼ cup water
- 1 tablespoon granulated sugar
- 1 ½ teaspoons kosher salt

- 1 large English cucumber, thinly sliced (about 1 pound)
- ½ red or sweet onion, cut into quarters and thinly sliced

DIRECTIONS

1. In a large bowl, whisk together the distilled white vinegar, water, granulated sugar, kosher salt, and coarse ground black pepper until the sugar and salt are dissolved.
2. Add the thinly sliced English cucumber and red or sweet onion to the bowl, tossing to coat the vegetables evenly with the dressing.
3. Cover the bowl with plastic wrap and refrigerate for at least 30 minutes to allow the flavors to meld and the vegetables to chill.
4. Serve the Classic Cucumber Salad chilled, garnished with fresh dill or parsley if desired.

Tips from the Homestead:

- The success of this recipe relies on the freshness and quality of the cucumbers and onions. Choose the best ingredients available for the best flavor and texture.
- Prepare the salad up to a day in advance, storing it in the refrigerator until serving.

DRY RANCH DRESSING MIX

INGREDIENTS

- 1/2 cup dried dill weed
- 1/2 cup dried parsley
- 1/4 cup dried onion flakes
- 1/4 cup onion powder
- 1/4 cup garlic powder
- 2 tablespoons dried chives
- 2 tablespoons salt
- 1 tablespoon black pepper

DIRECTIONS

1. In a large mixing bowl, combine the dried dill weed, dried parsley, dried onion flakes, onion powder, garlic powder, dried chives, salt, and black pepper.
2. Mix the ingredients until well combined, ensuring an even distribution of herbs and spices.
3. Store the Homemade Dry Ranch Dressing Mix in an airtight container at room temperature for up to 1 year.

*Swipe crumbs on floor

To Make Wet Ranch Dressing:

1. In a small bowl, whisk together 1/2 cup each of mayonnaise, milk, and sour cream.
2. Add 1 tablespoon of the Homemade Dry Ranch Dressing Mix to the wet ingredients and whisk until smooth.
3. Store the Wet Ranch Dressing in the refrigerator for up to 1 week.

Tips from the Homestead:

- Use this Homemade Dry Ranch Dressing Mix to make a variety of ranch-flavored dishes, such as dips, sauces, and marinades.
- Make ranch-flavored popcorn: Sprinkle a pinch of Homemade Dry Ranch Dressing Mix over freshly popped popcorn for a delicious and addictive snack.

FRENCH ONION DIP MIX

INGREDIENTS

- 3/4 cup dried minced onion
- 3 tablespoons dried parsley
- 4 teaspoons sea salt
- 2 teaspoons black pepper
- 2 teaspoons onion powder
- 1 teaspoon celery seed

DIRECTIONS

1. In a large mixing bowl, combine the dried minced onion, dried parsley, sea salt, black pepper, onion powder, and celery seed.
2. Mix the ingredients until they are fully incorporated and a uniform consistency is achieved.
3. Store the Homemade French Onion Dip Mix in an airtight container at room temperature for up to 6 months.

*Swipe crumbs on floor.

Usage:

To make a delicious French onion dip, simply mix 1 tablespoon of the Homemade French Onion Dip Mix with 1 cup of sour cream or yogurt. Refrigerate for at least 30 minutes to allow the flavors to meld.

Tips from the Homestead:

- Make your own ingredients to give a more in depth flavor.
- Incorporate into your favorite recipes, such as soups, stews, and casseroles, for an added boost of flavor.

Soups & Gravies

AU JUS MIX

INGREDIENTS

- 1/2 cup beef bouillon powder
- 1/2 tablespoon cornstarch
- 4 teaspoons onion powder
- 1/2 teaspoon garlic powder
- 1/2 teaspoon ground black pepper

DIRECTIONS

1. In a small bowl, combine the beef bouillon powder, cornstarch, onion powder, garlic powder, and black pepper.
2. Mix the ingredients until well combined, ensuring an even distribution of flavors.
3. Store the Homemade Au Jus Mix in an airtight container at room temperature for up to 6 months.

*Swipe crumbs on floor.

To Use:

- Add 2 tablespoons of the Homemade Au Jus Mix to 1 cup of hot water, whisking until smooth.

Tips from the Homestead:

- Use this Homemade Au Jus Mix to add depth and richness to your favorite roasts, stews, and soups.
- Use this Homemade Au Jus Mix as a base for your favorite French dip sandwiches, adding sliced roast beef and melted cheese for a hearty, satisfying meal.

BEEF INSPIRED BOUILLON

INGREDIENTS

- 4 tablespoons mushroom powder
- 4 tablespoons tomato powder
- 2 tablespoons sea salt
- 2 tablespoons nutritional yeast
- 2 tablespoons onion powder
- 2 tablespoons garlic powder

- 1 tablespoon mustard powder
- 1 tablespoon dried oregano
- 1 tablespoon ground black pepper
- 1 teaspoon celery seed
- 1 teaspoon parsley flakes

DIRECTIONS

1. In a small bowl, combine the mushroom powder, tomato powder, sea salt, nutritional yeast, onion powder, garlic powder, mustard powder, oregano, black pepper, celery seed, and parsley flakes.
2. Mix the ingredients until well combined, ensuring an even distribution of flavors.
3. Store the Homemade "Beef" Bouillon Powder in an airtight container at room temperature for up to 6 months.

*Swipe crumbs on floor.

To Use:

- Add 1 tablespoon of the Homemade "Beef" Bouillon Powder to 1 cup of hot water to create a savory broth.

Tips from the Homestead:

- Use this Homemade "Beef" Bouillon Powder to add depth and richness to your favorite soups, stews, and sauces.
- Experiment with adjusting the proportions of the ingredients to create customized flavor profiles.

BOUILLON POWDER

INGREDIENTS

- 2 cups nutritional yeast
- 4 tablespoons onion powder
- 4 tablespoons sea salt
- 3 teaspoons garlic powder
- 2 tablespoons dried parsley
- 2 tablespoons dill weed
- 2 teaspoons ground turmeric
- 2 teaspoons dried basil
- 2 teaspoons celery seed

DIRECTIONS

1. In a large bowl, combine the nutritional yeast, onion powder, sea salt, garlic powder, dried parsley, dill weed, ground turmeric, dried basil, and celery seed.
2. Mix the ingredients together until well combined, ensuring a uniform blend.
3. Store the Homemade Bouillon Powder in an airtight container, such as a glass jar with a tight-fitting lid. 6 month shelf life.

*Swipe crumbs on floor.

Usage:

Simply add 1 tablespoon of the powder to your recipe in place of one store-bought bouillon cube.

Tips from the Homestead:

• Adjust the amount of each ingredient to suit your personal taste preferences, creating a unique and delicious bouillon powder blend.
• Double or triple the recipe to make a larger batch of Homemade Bouillon Powder, ensuring a steady supply for future meals.

BROWN GRAVY MIX

INGREDIENTS

- 3 cups all-purpose flour
- 3/4 cup bouillon powder
- 2 teaspoons black pepper
- 2 teaspoons onion powder
- 2 teaspoons garlic powder
- 1 teaspoon paprika

DIRECTIONS

1. In a large mixing bowl, combine the all-purpose flour, bouillon powder, black pepper, onion powder, garlic powder, and paprika.
2. Mix the ingredients until they are fully incorporated and a uniform consistency is achieved.
3. Store the Homemade Brown Gravy Mix in an airtight container at room temperature for up to 6 months.

*Swipe crumbs on floor.

To Make Brown Gravy:

1. Measure 2 tablespoons of the Homemade Brown Gravy Mix (equivalent to 1 packet).
2. Mix the measured mix with 1 cup of hot water or broth, whisking continuously to avoid lumps.
3. Bring the mixture to a boil, then reduce the heat and simmer for 2-3 minutes, or until the gravy reaches your desired consistency.

Tips from the Homestead:

• Rub the Homemade Brown Gravy Mix onto roasted meats, such as beef or pork, for added flavor and aroma.

COUNTRY GRAVY MIX

INGREDIENTS

- 2 cups all-purpose flour
- 1 cup dry milk powder
- 1/4 cup cornstarch
- 1 tablespoon ground black pepper
- 1 tablespoon sea salt
- 1 tablespoon onion powder
- 1 teaspoon poultry seasoning

DIRECTIONS

1. In a large bowl, combine the flour, dry milk powder, cornstarch, black pepper, sea salt, onion powder, and poultry seasoning.
2. Mix the ingredients until well combined, ensuring an even distribution of flavors.
3. Store the Homemade Country Gravy Mix in an airtight container, such as a glass jar with a tight-fitting lid.

*Swipe crumbs on floor.

Storage and Shelf Life:

- Store the mix in a cool, dry place, away from direct sunlight and moisture.
- The mix will retain its flavor and texture for up to 6 months.

To Make Country Gravy:

1. Melt 2 tablespoons of lard or butter in a saucepan over medium heat.
2. Add 3 tablespoons of the Homemade Country Gravy Mix to the saucepan and cook for 3 minutes, stirring constantly.
3. Gradually add 1 cup of water or milk to the saucepan, whisking continuously until the gravy thickens.

CREAM OF ANYTHING BASE

INGREDIENTS

- 2 cups dry milk powder
- ¾ cup cornstarch
- 1 teaspoon onion powder
- 1 teaspoon garlic powder
- ½ teaspoon dried basil
- ½ teaspoon dried parsley
- ¼ teaspoon black pepper

DIRECTIONS

1. In a large mixing bowl, combine the dry milk powder, cornstarch, onion powder, garlic powder, dried basil, dried parsley, and black pepper.
2. Mix the ingredients until well combined, ensuring an even distribution of spices and powders.
3. Store the Cream of Anything in an airtight container at room temperature for up to 6 months.
*Swipe crumbs on floor.

Variations:
- Cream of Chicken: Mix 1/3 cup of the Homemade Cream of Anything Base with 1 1/4 cups of chicken broth. Whisk until smooth and bring to a boil over medium heat.
- Cream of Mushroom: Mix 1/3 cup of the Homemade Cream of Anything Base with 1 1/4 cups of water. Add 1/2 cup of cooked mushrooms or 1/4 cup of mushroom powder. Whisk until smooth and bring to a boil over medium heat.
- Cream of Broccoli: Mix 1/3 cup of the Homemade Cream of Anything Base with 1 1/4 cups of water. Add 1/2 cup of cooked broccoli. Whisk until smooth and bring to a boil over medium heat.

Tips from the Homestead:

- Use this Homemade Cream of Anything Base to create a variety of creamy sauces and soups, such as cream of tomato, cream of spinach, or cream of asparagus.

ONION SOUP MIX

INGREDIENTS

- 1 cup minced onion
- 1/2 cup beef bouillon powder
- 1 tablespoon onion powder
- 1 tablespoon dried parsley flakes
- 1 tablespoon brown sugar

- 2 teaspoons garlic powder
- 1 teaspoon ground black pepper
- 1 teaspoon smoked paprika
- 1/2 teaspoon celery seed
- 1/2 teaspoon salt

DIRECTIONS

1. In a large mixing bowl, combine the minced onion, beef bouillon powder, onion powder, dried parsley flakes, brown sugar, garlic powder, ground black pepper, smoked paprika, celery seed, and salt.
2. Mix the ingredients until they are fully incorporated and a uniform consistency is achieved.
3. Store the Homemade Onion Soup Mix in an airtight container at room temperature for up to 6 months.

*Swipe crumbs on floor.

Usage:

To make a delicious onion soup, simply mix 4 tablespoons of the Homemade Onion Soup Mix with 4 cups of hot water. Bring the mixture to a boil, then reduce the heat and simmer for 10-15 minutes, or until the soup has reached your desired consistency.

Tips from the Homestead:

- Mix the Homemade Onion Soup Mix into meatballs or burgers for added flavor and moisture.
- Dehydrate as many of the ingredients as you can for a more flavorful soup.

Spreads

APPLE BUTTER

INGREDIENTS

- 14 apples (any variety, cored and diced)
- 4 teaspoons ground cinnamon
- 1 teaspoon ground nutmeg
- 1/2 cup water

DIRECTIONS

1. Add the diced apples to an Instant Pot or pressure cooker.
2. Add the ground cinnamon, ground nutmeg, and water to the Instant Pot.
3. Close the lid and cook on high pressure for 20 minutes.
4. Perform a quick release to depressurize the Instant Pot.
5. Switch to sauté mode and cook for 5 minutes, stirring continuously.
6. Use an immersion blender to blend the mixture to your desired consistency.
7. Prepare pint-sized jars by heating them in a pot of simmering water.
8. Fill the heated jars with the apple butter mixture, leaving 1/4 inch of headspace.
9. Fingertip tighten the lids and wipe the rims with a clean, damp cloth.
10. Process the jars in a boiling water bath for 10 minutes to ensure proper canning and shelf stability.

Yield:

- This recipe yields 5 pint-sized jars of Homemade Apple Butter.

Tips from the Homestead:

- Use this Homemade Apple Butter as a spread on toast, biscuits, or scones.
- Add Homemade Apple Butter to your favorite recipes, such as muffins, cakes, or cookies.
- Experiment with different spice blends, such as adding ground ginger or allspice, to create unique flavor profiles.

HAZELNUT SPREAD

INGREDIENTS

- 2 cups dry roasted and peeled hazelnuts
- 1/3 cup powdered sugar
- 1/4 cup cocoa powder
- 2 tablespoons vanilla extract
- 2 tablespoons coconut oil
- 1/2 teaspoon sea salt

DIRECTIONS

1. In a high-powered blender or using an immersion blender, blend the hazelnuts until smooth and creamy.
2. Add the powdered sugar, cocoa powder, vanilla extract, coconut oil, and sea salt to the blender.
3. Blend the mixture until well combined and smooth, stopping to scrape down the sides of the blender as needed.

*Swipe crumbs on floor.

Storage and Shelf Life:

- Store the Homemade Hazelnut Spread in an airtight container at room temperature for up to 2 weeks.
- For longer storage, refrigerate the spread in an airtight container for up to 2 months.

Tips from the Homestead:

- Use this Homemade Hazelnut Spread as a delicious topping for toast, pancakes, or waffles.
- Experiment with adding different flavorings, such as cinnamon or nutmeg, to create unique variations.

PEANUT BUTTER

INGREDIENTS

- 1 pound organic roasted peanuts
- 2 tablespoons avocado oil (optional, but recommended for smoother blending)
- 1 teaspoon sea salt

DIRECTIONS

1. Combine the roasted peanuts, avocado oil (if using), and sea salt in a high-powered blender.
2. Blend the mixture on high speed until it reaches your desired consistency. For smooth peanut butter, continue blending until the mixture is creamy and uniform. For chunky peanut butter, stop the blender sooner, leaving a delightful texture of peanut pieces.

*Swipe crumbs on floor.

Storage and Shelf Life:
- Store in an airtight container such as a glass jar with a lid.
- 2 weeks on counter or 2 months in refrigerator.

Tips from the Homestead:

- For optimal flavor and nutrition, choose organic roasted peanuts that are free from additives and preservatives.
- If you find that your peanut butter is too thick, add a small amount of avocado oil or coconut oil to achieve the desired consistency.
- Homemade peanut butter makes a wonderful addition to your homestead pantry, and it's perfect for snacking, baking, or making sandwiches for your family. Enjoy!

STRAWBERRY JAM

INGREDIENTS

- 2 pounds fresh strawberries, hulled and sliced
- 1 cup granulated sugar
- 4 tablespoons freshly squeezed lemon juice

DIRECTIONS

1. In a large pot, combine the sliced strawberries and granulated sugar. Let it sit for about 15-20 minutes, until the strawberries start to release their juice and the mixture becomes syrupy.
2. Add the freshly squeezed lemon juice to the pot and stir to combine.
3. Bring the mixture to a boil over high heat, stirring occasionally.
4. Reduce the heat to medium-low and simmer the jam for about 20-25 minutes, or until it has thickened and passed the "wrinkle test".
5. Remove the pot from the heat and let the jam cool slightly.
6. Strain the jam through a food mill or a fine-mesh sieve to remove the seeds and achieve a smooth consistency.
7. Store in the refrigerator for up to 2 weeks.

Tips from the Homestead:

- Depending on the sweetness of your strawberries and your personal preference, you can adjust the amount of sugar to your taste.
- Experiment with adding a pinch of salt, a sprinkle of cinnamon, or a squeeze of fresh citrus juice to create unique and delicious variations on the classic recipe.

On The Stove

GRANDMAS FLOUR NOODLES

INGREDIENTS

- 4-6 cups all-purpose flour
- Poultry seasoning
- Pepper
- Water

DIRECTIONS

1. In a large mixing bowl, combine the flour, poultry seasoning, and pepper. Whisk until well combined.
2. Gradually add water to the dry ingredients, mixing until a smooth, pliable dough forms.
3. Knead the dough on a floured surface for 5-10 minutes, until it becomes elastic and smooth.
4. Roll out the dough to a thickness of approximately 1/4 inch (6 mm).
5. Use a pizza cutter or sharp knife to cut the dough into long, thin noodles.
6. Bring a large pot of chicken or beef stock to a boil.
7. Carefully add the homemade noodles to the boiling stock.
8. Cook the noodles for 5-6 minutes, or until they are tender but still firm to the bite.

Tips from the Homestead:

- Mix the dough just until the ingredients come together, avoiding overworking, which can lead to tough, dense noodles.

SPAGHETT SAUCE

INGREDIENTS

- Fresh tomatoes (any variety, such as Roma, Cherry, or Beefsteak)
- Garlic cloves
- Olive oil
- Fresh parsley
- Salt and pepper

DIRECTIONS

1. Preheat your oven to 400°F (200°C).
2. Cut the fresh tomatoes in half and place them cut-side up on a cookie sheet.
3. Scatter the garlic cloves throughout the tomatoes.
4. Sprinkle the fresh parsley, salt, and pepper over the tomatoes.
5. Drizzle the olive oil over the tomatoes, ensuring they are evenly coated.
6. Bake the tomatoes in the preheated oven for 35-40 minutes, or until they are tender and lightly caramelized.
7. Remove the tomatoes from the oven and allow them to cool slightly.
8. Transfer the tomatoes to a blender or food processor and blend until smooth.

Tips from the Homestead:

- Use fresh, high-quality ingredients: The flavor and quality of your Homemade Spaghetti Sauce will depend on the freshness and quality of your ingredients. Choose the best tomatoes, garlic, and parsley you can find.
- Roast the garlic for added depth: Roasting the garlic before adding it to the tomatoes will bring out its natural sweetness and add depth to the sauce.
- Acidity adjustment: If using tomatoes that are naturally sweet, you may want to add a splash of red wine or lemon juice to balance the acidity of the sauce.
- Make it a staple: Make a large batch of Homemade Spaghetti Sauce and can it or freeze it for future meals, ensuring a delicious and healthy sauce is always on hand.

Into The Oven

CORNBREAD

INGREDIENTS

- 1 cup cornmeal
- 1 cup all-purpose flour
- ⅔ cup granulated sugar
- 1 tablespoon baking powder
- ½ teaspoon salt
- 1 cup milk
- 2 eggs
- 1 can drained corn (15 ounces)
- ½ cup unsalted butter, melted

DIRECTIONS

1. Preheat your oven to 400°F (200°C).
2. Coat a square 8x8-inch baking pan or a cast-iron skillet with cooking spray.
3. In a large mixing bowl, combine the cornmeal, flour, sugar, baking powder, and salt. Whisk until well combined.
4. Add the milk, eggs, drained corn, and melted butter to the dry ingredients. Mix until just combined, being careful not to overmix.
5. Pour the cornbread batter into the prepared baking pan or cast-iron skillet.
6. Bake for 20-30 minutes, or until a toothpick inserted into the center of the cornbread comes out clean.
7. Remove the cornbread from the oven and let it cool for a few minutes before slicing and serving.

Tips from the Homestead:

- The quality of your cornbread will depend on the freshness and quality of your ingredients. Choose the best cornmeal, flour, and butter you can find.
- Mix the wet and dry ingredients just until combined. Overmixing can result in a dense and tough cornbread.

SOURDOUGH GOLDFISH

INGREDIENTS

- 120 grams all-purpose flour
- 3 grams salt
- 2 grams turmeric powder
- 100 grams sourdough starter (active or discard)
- 55 grams unsalted butter, softened
- 225 grams cheddar cheese, shredded

DIRECTIONS

1. Preheat your oven to 400°F (200°C).
2. Coat a square 8x8-inch baking pan or a cast-iron skillet with cooking spray.
3. In a large mixing bowl, combine the cornmeal, flour, sugar, baking powder, and salt. Whisk until well combined.
4. Add the milk, eggs, drained corn, and melted butter to the dry ingredients. Mix until just combined, being careful not to overmix.
5. Pour the cornbread batter into the prepared baking pan or cast-iron skillet.
6. Bake for 20-30 minutes, or until a toothpick inserted into the center of the cornbread comes out clean.
7. Remove the cornbread from the oven and let it cool for a few minutes before slicing and serving.

Tips from the Homestead:

- The quality of your cornbread will depend on the freshness and quality of your ingredients. Choose the best cornmeal, flour, and butter you can find.
- Mix the wet and dry ingredients just until combined. Overmixing can result in a dense and tough cornbread.

Home Remedies

ELECTROLYTE DRINK

INGREDIENTS

- 6 cups filtered water
- 3 tablespoons organic sugar
- 1 teaspoon sea salt

DIRECTIONS

1. In a large pitcher, combine the filtered water, organic sugar, and sea salt.
2. Mix the ingredients until the sugar and salt are fully dissolved.
3. Store the Homemade Electrolyte Drink in the refrigerator for up to 3 days.

Important Notice:

• As with any health-related remedy, consult with a medical professional before using this Homemade Electrolyte Drink, especially if you have any underlying health conditions.

Tips from the Homestead:

• Use this Homemade Electrolyte Drink to replenish essential electrolytes during or after intense physical activity, illness, or in hot weather.
• Experiment with adding slices of lemon, lime, or orange to the drink for added flavor and nutrition.

GARLIC & HONEY TINCTURE

INGREDIENTS

- 1 cup peeled and chopped garlic cloves
- 1 cup raw, local honey

DIRECTIONS

1. Chop 1 cup of garlic cloves and add them to a clean, sterilized jar.
2. Pour 1 cup of raw, local honey over the garlic cloves, ensuring they are completely covered.
3. Mix the garlic and honey together, then store the jar in a cool, dark place.
4. Loosen the lid daily for 2 weeks to allow any built-up gases to escape, tightening the lid after each release.
5. The longer the mixture steeps, the stronger the tincture will become.

Usage:

- Once the tincture has steeped, you can consume the honey directly or eat the garlic cloves.
- Use the Garlic Honey Tincture as a natural remedy for colds, coughs, and sore throats.
- Add the tincture to your favorite recipes for an extra boost of flavor and nutrition.

Tips from the Homestead:

- Use high-quality ingredients: Ensure the garlic is fresh and the honey is raw and local for optimal flavor and nutritional benefits.
- Adjust the steeping time: Steep the mixture for a shorter or longer period, depending on your desired level of potency.

MULLEIN LEAF TINCTURE

INGREDIENTS

- Fresh mullein leaves
- 100-proof vodka
- Quart-sized glass jar with lid

DIRECTIONS

1. Harvest fresh mullein leaves, selecting those with no signs of damage or discoloration.
2. Rinse the leaves gently with clean water to remove any dirt or debris. Pat the leaves dry with a clean towel to remove excess moisture.
3. Tear the mullein leaves into smaller pieces and fill the quart-sized glass jar, leaving about 1-2 inches of space at the top.
4. Pour 100-proof vodka over the mullein leaves, filling the jar to the top.
5. Store the jar in a dark, cool place, such as a pantry or cupboard. Shake the jar daily for 6-8 weeks to facilitate the infusion process.
6. After 6-8 weeks, strain the tincture through a cheesecloth or a potato ricer into clean amber glass bottles. Discard the solids.
7. Take the mullein tincture daily via a dropper, following the recommended dosage.

Tips from the Homestead:

- Always identify mullein leaves correctly to avoid confusion with other plants.
- Keep the tincture away from children and pets.
- Consult with a healthcare professional before using mullein tincture, especially if you have any underlying medical conditions.

By following this simple recipe, you can create a potent and effective mullein tincture to support your health and wellness goals.

Homesteading

CRANBERRY JUICE

INGREDIENTS

- Fresh or frozen cranberries
- Granulated sugar (or honey, to taste)
- Water

DIRECTIONS

1. Wash the cranberries thoroughly and pick out any stems or debris.
2. Sterilize the quart jars, lids, and rings in boiling water for 10-15 minutes.
3. Pack 1 1/2 cups of cranberries into each quart jar.
4. Add 1/2 cup of granulated sugar (or honey, to taste) to each jar. You can adjust the amount of sugar to your taste preferences.
5. Fill the remaining space in the jars with boiling water, leaving a 1-inch headspace.
6. Use a paper towel to dry the rims of the jars, then apply the lids and rings fingertip tight.
7. Process the jars in a boiling water bath for 25 minutes, adjusting for altitude as necessary.
8. Remove the jars from the water bath and let them sit undisturbed for 24 hours.
9. After 24 hours, remove the rings and check the seals. Store the sealed jars in a cool, dark place for up to 6-8 weeks before consuming.

Tips from the Homestead:

- You can adjust the amount of sugar to your taste preferences. If using honey, keep in mind that it has a stronger flavor than sugar.

RENDERING LARD

INGREDIENTS

- 5 pounds pork fat
- 1 cup water

DIRECTIONS

1. Cut the pork fat into manageable chunks to ensure even rendering.
2. Place the chunks of pork fat into the crockpot. Add 1 cup of water to the crockpot.
3. Set the crockpot to the low setting and cook for 4-6 hours. The exact cooking time will depend on the size of the fat chunks.
4. Regularly check on the lard and stir it to prevent burning. You want to achieve a clear, golden liquid.
5. Once the fat has fully rendered, carefully pour the hot lard through cheesecloth or a clean, thin towel into a heat-resistant container. Discard the solids or make crackling.

Storage and Shelf Life:

- Store the lard in an airtight container in the refrigerator for several months or freeze for longer-term storage.

Tips from the Homestead:

- Use high-quality pork fat from pasture-raised pigs for the best flavor and nutritional profile.
- Experiment with using lard in traditional recipes, such as pie crusts, biscuits, and fried chicken.
- Consider rendering lard in bulk and storing it in smaller containers for convenient use in future recipes.

WATERGLASS EGGS

INGREDIENTS

- Unwashed fresh eggs
- Pickling lime (calcium hydroxide)
- Fresh water
- 1/2 gallon jar with lid
- Quart-sized jar

DIRECTIONS

1. Carefully place the unwashed fresh eggs, pointy side down, into the 1/2 gallon jar.
2. In the quart-sized jar, combine fresh water and 3 tablespoons of pickling lime. Shake the jar vigorously to dissolve the lime.
3. Pour the lime-water mixture over the eggs, filling the jar to the rim.
4. Secure the lid tightly
5. Store the jar in a cool, dark place, maintaining a consistent temperature between 40°F and 70°F (4°C and 21°C).

Shelf Life:

Eggs preserved using the water glass method can be stored for 18-24 months, providing a reliable source of protein during times of scarcity.

Tips from the Homestead:

- The quality of the eggs will directly impact the success of the preservation method. Choose fresh, clean eggs from your backyard flock or a local farm.
- Store the jar in a cool, dark place, away from direct sunlight and heat sources, to ensure the eggs remain preserved and safe to eat.
- Check the eggs periodically for signs of spoilage, such as an off smell or slimy texture. Remove and discard any spoiled eggs to maintain the integrity of the remaining eggs.

KITCHEN ESSENTIALS

I'm excited to share my personal favorite kitchen essentials that have proven indispensable in my own homesteading journey. The best part? You don't need to break the bank by buying everything new. Thrifting, auctions, and online marketplaces can be a great way to get started.

Must-Have Kitchen Tools

1. Danish Dough Whisk: A versatile and durable tool perfect for mixing and blending dough, batter, and other thick mixtures.
2. Dehydrator: A game-changer for preserving fruits, vegetables, and herbs, allowing you to enjoy your harvest year-round.
3. Jars, Rings, and Lids: Essential for canning and storing your homemade goodies. Look for deals at auctions, thrift stores, or online marketplaces.
4. Jar Funnels: A simple but handy tool that makes filling jars a breeze, reducing mess and waste.
5. Immersion Blender: Perfect for soups, sauces, and other liquids, this handy blender saves time and effort.
6. Crock Pot: A staple for any homesteader, allowing you to cook hearty meals while you tend to other tasks.
7. Mixing Bowls: Invest in a set of durable, easy-to-clean mixing bowls, such as vintage Pyrex.
8. Mixer (Hand or Stand): A reliable mixer is a must-have for any homesteader, making quick work of tasks like baking and whipping.
9. Water Bath Canner: Essential for safely canning high-acid foods like jams, jellies, and pickles.
10. Jar Tongs: A handy tool for lifting hot jars out of the canner or off the shelf, reducing the risk of burns and breakage.

Thrifty Tips

• Don't be afraid to get creative and repurpose items you already have on hand.

By investing in these essential kitchen tools and adopting a thrifty mindset, you'll be well on your way to becoming a successful homesteader. Happy cooking!

KEY SUBSTITUTIONS

As a homesteader, you understand the importance of being prepared and resourceful in the kitchen. Sometimes, key ingredients may be scarce or unavailable, but with these clever substitutions, you can continue to cook and bake with confidence.

Dairy Substitutions
1. Buttermilk Substitute: 1 tablespoon lemon juice or vinegar + 1 cup milk
2. Half-and-Half Substitute: 1 tablespoon melted butter + 1 cup milk
3. Heavy Cream Substitute: 1/3 cup milk + 3 tablespoons melted butter
4. Milk Substitute: 1/2 cup evaporated milk + 1/2 cup water

Baking Substitutions
1. Baking Powder Substitute: 1/2 teaspoon cream of tartar + 1/2 teaspoon baking soda
2. Brown Sugar Substitute: 1 cup sugar + 1 tablespoon molasses

Pantry Substitutions
1. Tomato Sauce Substitute: 1/2 cup tomato paste + 1/2 cup water
2. Broth Substitute: 1 cup water + 1 tablespoon soy sauce
3. Honey Substitute: 1 1/4 cups sugar + 1/4 cup water

Egg Substitutions
1. Egg Substitute: 1/2 banana or 1/4 cup applesauce

By incorporating these ingredient substitutions into your cooking and baking repertoire, you'll be better equipped to handle unexpected ingredient shortages and continue to create delicious, homemade meals for your family. Happy cooking!

KITCHEN CONVERSION CHART

LIQUID MEASURES

FLUID OZ	CUP	PINT	QUART	GALLON
8	1	1/2	1/4	1/16
16	2	1	1/2	1/8
32	4	2	1	1/4
64	8	4	2	1/2
128	16	8	4	1

DRY MEASURES

GRAM	TEASPOON	TABLESPOON	CUP
14	3	1	1/16
29	6	2	1/8
57	12	4	1/4
114	24	8	1/2
171	36	12	3/4
229	48	16	1

OVEN TEMPERATURES

°C	120	160	180	205	220
°F	250	320	350	400	425

NOTES

NOW GO SWIPE SOME
CRUMBS ON THE FLOOR